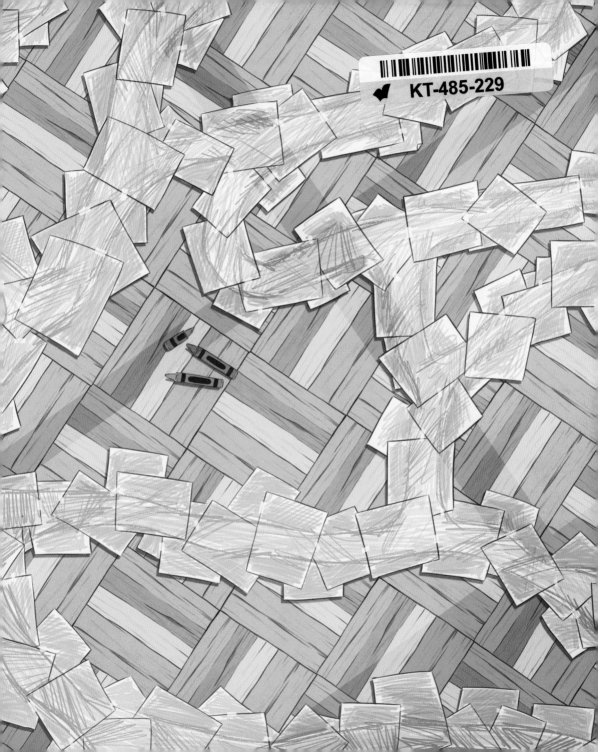

STRANGER THINGS
FIELD GUIDE

STRANGER THINGS
FIELD GUIDE

⊨ NADIA BAILEY ⊨

illustrated by Phil Constantinesco

**Smith
Street
Books**

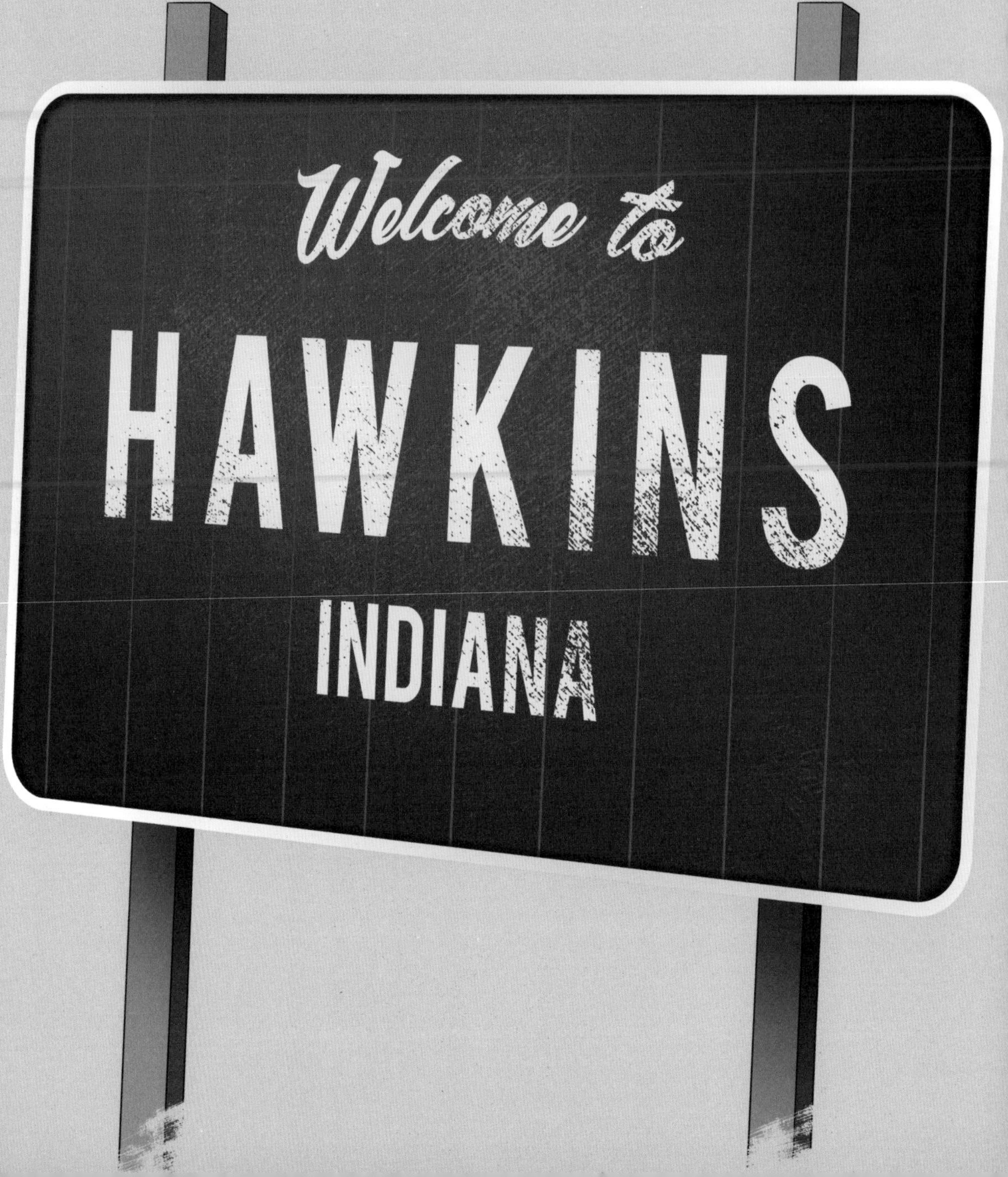
Welcome to
HAWKINS
INDIANA

HAWKINS CITY COUNCIL COMMUNITY CHRISTMAS MEMO, DEC 1984

Hello everyone, and Merry Christmas from your friends at Hawkins
City Council. This has been a big year for Hawkins. We were saddened
by the loss of Barbara Holland last year, but, thanks to the work
of anonymous whistleblowers, we now know the truth behind her very
tragic death and trust that those responsible for this tragedy will
be brought to justice. Our thoughts and prayers are with her family
and friends.

We would also like to pay tribute to Bob Newby, an upstanding
Hawkins citizen and employee of Radio Shack, who tragically lost
his life while exploring some dangerous caves close to the Hawkins
National Laboratory. We would urge all Hawkins residents to steer
clear of these caves and tunnels. Mr Newby was a very well-liked
member of the Hawkins community and his loss is felt keenly by
his family and friends.

A special thanks to Chief Jim Hopper and the whole squad at Hawkins
Police Department for their continued work to protect and serve the
community. I think we all agree that we have some of the finest
people on the job.

Congratulations to Hawkins High School's graduating class of '84,
and a special message of support to our Middle School students who
are anticipating this year's Snow Ball. Have a dance for us, kids.

Regards,

HAWKINS CITY COUNCILLORS

1984

THE BOY WHO CAME BACK TO LIFE

William Byers found safe, but questions remain surrounding his disappearance, supposed death and subsequent 'autopsy'.

In spite of being laid to rest last month, Hawkins Middle School student William Byers has been found alive and well. The 12-year-old son of Hawkins resident Joyce Byers and her former husband, Lonnie Byers, was reported missing after he failed to return home on 6 November 1983. William's bike was found at the intersection of Cornwallis and Kerley streets, known to some locals as 'Mirkwood', prompting fears that he had been abducted.

Several days later, the body of a young boy around William's age was discovered in the Sattler Quarry. An autopsy confirmed his identity as William Byers and that he had died by drowning. No foul play was suspected, despite the vocal protests of Mrs Byers that the body was not her son's. The grief-stricken mother declined to be interviewed at the time.

William Byers' funeral was held a few days later, attended by his family, fellow students and members of the Hawkins Middle School faculty. He was buried in Hawkins Cemetery – or so we were led to believe.

Last week, William Byers was admitted to the general hospital suffering exposure and malnutrition, but very much alive.

This mystery is just one of many strange happenings that have afflicted the town in recent weeks. The tragic suicide of Benny Hammond, owner of Benny's Burgers, and the disappearance of Hawkins High School student Barbara Holland are just two such events that have shaken our small community. So too are the rumours surrounding the highly-guarded Hawkins National Laboratory.

When asked for an interview by this newspaper, a spokesperson from the Dept. of Energy declined to comment.

Speaking to our reporters earlier today, Chief Jim Hopper expressed gratitude that William Byers had been found and asked that people respect the Byers family's privacy.

'This has been a terrible time for all of us,' Chief Hopper said. 'And the last thing the family needs is for you lot to be harassing them for comments.'

'The most important thing is that Will's home safe with his family,' he continued. 'Let's just leave it at that.'

When Mrs Byers was asked about the mysterious circumstances regarding her son's disappearance and return, she said, 'We're just so happy … so happy … that Will has come back to us'.

Her older son, Jonathan Byers, expressed similar sentiments: 'Will is safe and that's all that matters,' he said. 'Now please leave us alone.'

The Hawkins Police Force have urged citizens with any information on the child John Doe, misidentified as Will Byers, to come forward. More updates on this strange story as it develops.

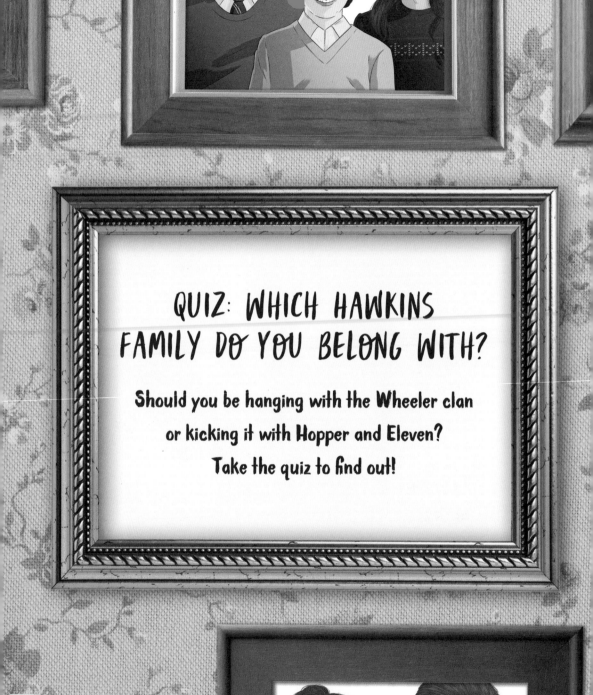

QUIZ: WHICH HAWKINS FAMILY DO YOU BELONG WITH?

Should you be hanging with the **Wheeler** clan
or kicking it with **Hopper** and **Eleven**?
Take the quiz to find out!

HOW DO YOU FEEL ABOUT YOUR FATHER?

a) He's kind of a deadbeat.

b) He's fine, but he's so boring.

c) I hate him.

d) It's complicated.

GOOD MORNING! WHAT'S FOR BREAKFAST?

a) Something simple, like scrambled eggs on toast.

b) A big spread with all the trimmings: bacon, eggs, pancakes with lots of syrup, orange juice, coffee, the works.

c) Breakfast hasn't been the same since your parents divorced.

d) Eggos. Also, coffee.

WHAT ABOUT YOUR MOM?

a) She's highly strung, but I love her.

b) She should never have married my dad.

c) She's a pushover.

d) It's complicated.

YOU WANT TO BUY SOME NEW CLOTHES. HOW DO YOUR PARENTS REACT?

a) Money's too tight right now.

b) Done. It's time to hit the mall.

c) You need to fix your attitude before you ask for new clothes.

d) Your new clothes will be thrifted, but they'll be chosen with love.

YOU INTRODUCE YOUR CRUSH TO YOUR PARENTS. HOW DO THEY RESPOND?

a) Honestly, you wish they'd chill out. They're a little too excited.

b) They're polite, but they're privately judging your choices.

c) Are you kidding? You would never bring a date home.

d) Oh no, you're about to get 'the talk'.

YOU MESS UP AND GET INTO TROUBLE. HOW DO YOUR PARENTS REACT?

a) With sympathy. They know you're a good kid at heart.

b) With disbelief. They raised you better than this.

c) With resignation. They knew you were a bad seed all along.

d) With anger. But it's tempered with love.

WHAT'S YOUR HOUSE LIKE?

a) It's a bit old and shabby but, hey, it's home.

b) Comfortable. Your parents like their mod cons.

c) It sucks, just like the whole town sucks.

d) It's got ... loads of character.

HOW DO YOU PARENTS REACT IN A CRISIS?

a) They may seem a little bit crazy, but it's only because they're so worried.

b) They take a step back and let the police or government deal with it.

c) They assume you're the cause of the problem.

d) They remain calm and do whatever it takes to protect you.

Mostly As: YOU BELONG WITH...

The Byers Family

They might not be perfect, but you're lucky enough to belong to a family who really, really love one another. You've seen some tough times – whether that's money trouble, a deadbeat dad or a brother afflicted with supernatural possession – but that's only brought your fam closer together. And your mom's new boyfriend? Sure, he's a super nerd, but it turns out he's one of the good ones.

Mostly Bs: *YOU BELONG WITH ...*

the Wheeler Family

Congratulations, you belong with one of Hawkins'
most well-respected families. Your upbringing has been
comfortable and you've never really wanted for anything
— except maybe more excitement in your life. Your parents
think they know best when it comes to your future, but you
have an inkling you want to make different choices. Don't
let that comfortable life lull you into a false sense of
security: there's a whole world out there.

Mostly Cs: *YOU BELONG WITH ...*

the Hargrove-Mayfield Family

It's hard being the child of divorced parents. It's even harder trying to make things work when your olds remarry – and suddenly you've got a new brother or sister who you never asked for and certainly don't want. Your parents are the kind of people who favour a 'tough love' approach, which sometimes veers into plain meanness. It's hard to love a family who you feel doesn't love you, but try to hang in there. It gets better.

Mostly Ds: *YOU BELONG WITH ...*

the Hopper Family

Your upbringing's been ... complicated. It's tough coming from an unusual background, even tougher trying to find your way in a world that's consistently done you wrong. You're lucky enough to have found a parental figure who genuinely cares for you. Who wants the best for you. Who'll do anything to protect you. Keep testing those boundaries, but never forget that you're loved. You're one of the lucky ones.

ELEVEN

CHARACTER PROFILE: ELEVEN / JANE IVES

Abducted from her mother, Terry Ives, and raised in seclusion at the Hawkins National Laboratory, Eleven's early upbringing can be best described as bleak. Possessing extraordinary psychic abilities, she was denied a proper childhood and was instead the prized test subject of Dr Martin Brenner. But after an experiment gone awry allowed her to escape the Lab and take refuge with Mike Wheeler, her true character began to emerge: smart, loyal and resourceful, with more psychic gifts than Dr Brenner had imagined. While her difficult childhood left her with only a basic understanding of social cues and a tendency to angrily lash out when things don't go her way, she deeply values the people who've shown her kindness and is making tentative steps towards building a normal life -- or as normal as you can be when you have the ability to flip over a van using only the power of your mind.

GET EL'S LOOK

THE RUNAWAY

Even when she's just emerged from the perils of the Void and escaped from Hawkins National Laboratory, Eleven is always serving a strong look. Practical? No. Stylish? Also no. But when you're a telekinetic pre-teen with a psychic axe to grind, sometimes you have to make do with what you've got.

BUZZ-CUT HAIR, ALL THE BETTER FOR ATTACHING ELECTRODES TO

FOR ALL OF YOUR CAN-CRUSHING NEEDS

A JAZZY SNOWFLAKE PATTERN IS ONE WAY TO MAKE A HOSPITAL GOWN FEEL LESS MISERABLE

⪤ Eleven: ⪥

A Psychic Primer

Eleven's psychic abilities are mysterious and varied. Her primary powers are psychokinesis and telekinesis. Her abilities also include biokinesis and ESP.

What is the origin of Eleven's powers?

While the exact source of Eleven's powers is as yet unknown, we know it has something to do with her mother, Terry Ives, who was a test subject in the MKUltra program. While Terry was pregnant, Dr Martin Brenner subjected her to a number of sensory deprivation experiments via immersion in an isolation tank, while also under the influence of psychedelic drugs. Although it is unconfirmed, these experiments are believed to have somehow caused Eleven's psychic abilities.

What is psychokinesis?

Psychokinesis is the ability to manipulate objects using the power of the mind, with no physical intervention. The word was coined in 1914 and is derived from the Greek words meaning *mind* and *movement*. Eleven's psychokinetic feats include crushing a soda can, slamming and locking doors and manipulating compass points to direct away from the Gate.

What is telekinesis?

Telekinesis is considered to be a form of psychokinesis, and means the ability to move objects using the power of the mind, with no physical intervention. The word was coined in 1890, and is derived from the Greek words meaning *distance* and *movement*. Eleven uses her telekinetic powers to make a model of the Millennium Falcon float in the air, pull a skateboard out from under Max and flip a Hawkins National Laboratory van.

What is biokinesis?

Biokinesis is the psychic manipulation of living things. Some of Eleven's more violent acts, such as breaking Hawkins Middle School student Troy's arm, killing Hawkins National Laboratory guards and nearly choking Ray Carroll to death, are examples of her biokinetic abilities.

What is ESP?

ESP stands for extrasensory perception and means the ability to acquire information through the mind, rather than the physical senses. It's also sometimes known as the 'sixth sense' or 'second sight'. Eleven displayed her extrasensory abilities when she recognised Will in a photo even though she'd never seen him, sent her consciousness to other places to learn new information and transmitted the voices of distant people over radio waves.

Trivia

Project MKUltra really existed. The Central Intelligence Agency (CIA) began the project in the early 1950s with the goal of developing mind-altering substances, which could be used to secretly control human behaviour. Justified by Cold War paranoia, MKUltra's researchers administered hallucinogenic drugs and subjected participants to hypnosis, sensory deprivation, isolation and verbal abuse, often without their knowledge or consent. The program was abruptly terminated in 1973, and CIA Director Richard Helms ordered all MKUltra files to be destroyed.

HAWKINS HIGH
STUDENT NEWSLETTER

◇◇

A weekly update from the Senior School Council,
bringing YOU the student news that matters.

◇◇

FRIGHT NIGHT: GET READY FOR HALLOWEEN

Calling all werewolves, witches and weirdos: it's time to get spooky for Halloween! This year, we are looking beyond the obvious costume choices and suggesting that you ditch the vampire fangs in favour of something with a little more class. Take it from senior student Nancy Wheeler, who hinted that her costume will be inspired by one of the year's coolest films. 'Let's just say that me and Steve have been planning it for weeks,' she said. 'It's gonna be great.' How intriguing! Whatever you decide on, make sure you save it for Halloween night. No matter how great your costume is, wearing it on a school day is for dweebs. You've been warned!

MR CLARKE'S FUN SCIENCE FACTS

DID YOU KNOW? ...

... that NASA's Pioneer 10 spacecraft, which left Earth on 2 March 1972, passed Neptune last year, making it the first human-made object to exist beyond the major planets of the solar system?

... that it's possible to build your own computer? The Yugoslavian popular science magazine *Galaksija* published a special issue in January, which details exactly how to do it. The only catch? The instructions are in Serbian!

... that Neptune might have rings? In 1846, the astronomer William Lassell observed what he thought was a ring around the planet (he also discovered Neptune's largest moon, the mighty Triton). Now, a team at La Silla Observatory have new evidence to support the theory: two separate scans have given evidence for ring-like arcs around the planet!

Mr Clarke's quote of the day:

'The moving power of mathematical invention is not reasoning but imagination.'

AUGUSTUS DE MORGAN (1806–1871)

WELCOME TO HAWKINS ...

It's time to welcome two new students into our midst! We caught up with step-siblings Billy Hargrove and Maxine Mayfield and got them to answer a couple of questions ...

Billy is a Hawkins senior student with a love of fast cars and rock'n'roll – and he's already proven very popular with the ladies. Get to know him below ...

Name: Billy

Age: 17

Favourite subject: Free period

Favourite thing about Hawkins High School: The girls

Theme song: Metallica – 'The Four Horsemen'

Voted most likely to: Steal your girl

Signature outfit: Are you serious? Levis, I guess.

Most treasured possession: My car

Person you most admire: Steve Harrington. I hear he's the King.

What you want to be when you grow up: Rich

Meet Maxine, the newest kid on the Middle School block. Don't be fooled by her prickly exterior – we think this strawberry-haired tomboy secretly has a heart of gold.

Name: Do not call me Maxine. It's Max.

Age: 13

Favourite subject: They all suck

Favourite thing about Hawkins High School: Leaving it

Theme song: Joan Jett and the Blackhearts – 'Crimson and Clover'

Voted most likely to: Kick your ass for asking dumb questions

Signature outfit: Clothes

Most treasured possession: My skateboard

Person you most admire: The guy who invented skateboards

What you want to be when you grow up: Away from here

DONATION DRIVE

The Senior School Council is holding a bake sale next weekend to raise funds to assist the Holland family in their ongoing search for their daughter, missing senior Barbara Holland. The sale will be held outside Melvald's General Store between 9 am and 3 pm, and all proceeds will be donated to the Holland family. We hear that Doris is going to make her famous black forest pie! For all enquiries, please contact Nancy Wheeler.

SAVE THE DATE:
HAWKINS MIDDLE SNOW BALL '84

Don't forget, Middle School students – the annual Snow Ball is only a few weeks away! The Middle School Social Committee is working hard to make this year's ball the best one yet. If you'd like to be involved in putting on this much-anticipated event, please contact Jennifer Hayes. Tickets are available from the front office. And remember: it's never too soon to ask that special someone to be your date. See you on the dance floor!

MIKE

CHARACTER PROFILE: MIKE WHEELER

Mike Wheeler is the son of Ted and Karen Wheeler and the middle sibling between Nancy and Holly. He's grown up in a pretty happy and secure home, which gives him a natural sense of confidence and a strong understanding of right and wrong. He's deeply loyal to his best friends Will, Dustin and Lucas, with whom he shares a sacred oath -- friends don't lie -- and, as Dungeon Master, is the unofficial leader of their party. He formed an instant bond with Eleven after finding her in the woods and sheltering her in his home, which has only strengthened over time: 'I never gave up on you,' he says when they're finally reunited after a whole year apart. 'I called you every night. Every night!'

CHIEF JIM HOPPER'S TRIPLE DECKER EGGO EXTRAVAGANZA

Only 8000 calories!

Prep time: 10 minutes   Serves: 2

INGREDIENTS

3 Eggo Homestyle Waffles

1 can of whipped cream

as many Hershey's Kisses as you can handle

1 big handful of jellybeans

a sprinkling of Reese's Pieces

METHOD

Pop the Eggos in the toaster until they're warm and delicious. Remove them and stack on a plate.

On a separate plate, squeeze out a circle of whipped cream. Top it with a mix of Hershey's Kisses, jellybeans and Reese's Pieces according to your preference, then place your first Eggo on top. Cover it with cream and candy. Repeat this process in layers until you've used all three Eggos. Top the final Eggo with extra cream and a liberal sprinkling of candy.

To serve, cut in half. Best shared with someone you love.

HAVE YOU SEEN THIS GIRL?

If spotted, do not approach. Please notify Chief Jim Hopper at the Hawkins Police Department immediately.

CHAPTER 1:
THE VANISHING OF WILL BYERS

6 November 1983. Hawkins, Indiana ... On the way home from his friend Mike Wheeler's house, Will Byers is stalked by something terrifying, then disappears. Nancy Wheeler and Barbara Holland discuss Nancy's love life. Nancy and Steve Harrington make out. Joyce Byers reports Will's disappearance to Chief Jim Hopper but isn't taken seriously. A mysterious girl with a shaved head shows up at Benny's Burgers -- but before Benny can find out her story, some people claiming to be from Child Protection Services show up and kill him in cold blood. They try to catch the girl, but she uses her telekinetic powers to escape. Mike, Dustin Henderson and Lucas Sinclair go looking for Will in the woods but find something else entirely ...

MONSTERS	✓	KISSING	✓
FLASHBACK	✓	TELEKINESIS	✓
NOSEBLEED	✗	BARB	✓

MUSICAL MOMENT

'White Rabbit' by Jefferson Airplane, playing on the radio at Benny's Burgers when Dr Brenner and his minions show up.

TRIVIA

The font used in the *Stranger Things* title sequence is called ITC Benguiat. It's also the typeface used for many of Stephen King's novels and the *Choose Your Own Adventure* series.

MEMORABLE QUOTE

'Mornings are for coffee and contemplation.' -- Jim Hopper

CHAPTER 2:
THE WEIRDO ON MAPLE STREET

Lucas, Mike and Dustin try to talk to Eleven, the girl they found in the woods. Hopper questions an anxious Joyce about a creepy phone call she received. Eleven shares information about Will's whereabouts. Barb and Nancy go to a pool party at Steve's house, which ends in a terrifying abduction.

MONSTERS	✓	KISSING	✓
FLASHBACK	✓	TELEKINESIS	✓
NOSEBLEED	✓	BARB	✓

MUSICAL MOMENT

'Should I Stay Or Should I Go' by The Clash -- a song with special significance to Jonathan and Will becomes a terrifying soundtrack to Joyce's encounter with the Demogorgon.

TRIVIA

The title of this episode is thought to be a nod to 'The Monsters Are Due on Maple Street', an episode of the classic sci-fi series *The Twilight Zone*.

MEMORABLE QUOTE

'Is that a new bra?' -- Barbara Holland

CHAPTER 3: HOLLY, JOLLY

Barb gets pulled into the Upside Down. Steve and Nancy go all the way. Chief Hopper gains access to Hawkins National Laboratory. Joyce is convinced Will is trying to communicate with her. Steve and Jonathan have a confrontation. Mike, Dustin, Lucas and Eleven continue to search for Will. An increasingly concerned Nancy looks for Barb. The police find Will's body in the Sattler Quarry ... or do they?

MONSTERS	✓	KISSING	✓
FLASHBACK	✓	TELEKINESIS	✓
NOSEBLEED	✓	BARB	✓

MUSICAL MOMENT

'Heroes' by Peter Gabriel (a towering orchestral version of the David Bowie original), heard playing as Hopper and the kids find out what has been discovered at the lake.

TRIVIA

Holly Wheeler is actually played by twins, Anniston and Tinsley Price. A lot of their reactions in the show were not scripted but improvised.

MEMORABLE QUOTE

'So do you think Eleven was born with her superpowers like the X-Men or do you think she acquired them like Green Lantern?' -- Dustin Henderson

CHAPTER 4: THE BODY

Joyce refuses to believe that Will is dead. Eleven uses
her powers to prove to the gang that Will is alive. They
subsequently give her a makeover so they can smuggle her
into school. Nancy and Jonathan form an unlikely alliance.
Hopper takes matters into his own hands and discovers
Will's body is not what it seems. Joyce has another
encounter with the horrors of the Upside Down.

MONSTERS	✓	KISSING	✗
FLASHBACK	✓	TELEKINESIS	✓
NOSEBLEED	✓	BARB	✗

MUSICAL MOMENT

'Atmosphere' by Joy Division -- a suitably bleak song to
soundtrack Jonathan's pain at losing his little brother.

TRIVIA

The reason the show looks so authentically of the era is
that the show's colourist, Skip Kimball, added a layer of
scanned '80s film-grain on top of the footage to achieve
a vintage film look.

MEMORABLE QUOTE

'Will is calling to me! And he's out there, and he's
alone, and he's scared, and I don't care if anyone
believes me!' -- Joyce Byers

CHAPTER 5:
THE FLEA AND THE ACROBAT

Hopper breaks into the Lab, but before he can complete his investigation, he's knocked out. Nancy and Jonathan decide to team up and go searching the woods for Will and Barb. The boys ask Mr Clarke how to travel to another dimension and, following a nifty explainer on how a space-time tear could create a gate into the Upside Down, hatch a plan to use their compasses to find the entrance. The plan is foiled by Eleven, causing a rift in the group. Nancy and Jonathan figure out where to find the Demogorgon, and Nancy unwittingly finds her way into the Upside Down.

MONSTERS	✓	KISSING	✗
FLASHBACK	✓	TELEKINESIS	✓
NOSEBLEED	✓	BARB	✗

MUSICAL MOMENT

'Nocturnal Me' by Echo & The Bunnymen, which soundtracks Jonathan's desperate search for Nancy.

TRIVIA

This is the first episode where the Upside Down is mentioned by name.

MEMORABLE QUOTE

'Science is neat ... But I'm afraid it's not very forgiving.' -- Mr Clarke

CHAPTER 6: THE MONSTER

Nancy escapes the Upside Down by following Jonathan's
voice and the two of them seek shelter at Nancy's house.
Steve goes looking for her and discovers what he assumes
is a tryst. Hopper and Joyce uncover the truth about the
Lab's experiments. The boys try to mend the rift caused
by Eleven's interference, but Lucas isn't having it.
Hopper and Joyce follow a lead to a woman they believe
to be Eleven's mother. Jonathan has a run-in with Steve
and, following a physical confrontation, Jonathan is
taken into custody. While Lucas follows a lead to
Hawkins National Laboratory, Mike, Dustin and Eleven
are confronted by a school bully, leading to a dramatic
demonstration of Eleven's powers. The trio return to
Mike's house, but they've been spotted ...

MONSTERS	✓	KISSING	✗
FLASHBACK	✓	TELEKINESIS	✓
NOSEBLEED	✓	BARB	✗

MUSICAL MOMENT

'Sunglasses at Night' by Corey Hart, which plays while
Steve tries to sneak into Nancy's room. (For the record,
Steve would *definitely* wear sunglasses at night.)

TRIVIA

The terrifying look of the Upside Down was partly inspired
by the paintings of Polish artist Zdzisław Beksiński. The
artist, although he had no formal training, became known
for painting otherworldly, hellish landscapes, featuring
strange figures and unearthly architecture.

MEMORABLE QUOTE

'You better run! She's our friend, and she's crazy!'
-- Dustin Henderson

CHAPTER 7: THE BATHTUB

Lucas warns Mike, Dustin and Eleven that 'the bad men are coming'. They bike up and escape -- meeting up with Lucas on the way -- before Eleven uses her powers to flip a van and ditch the bad guys for the time being. Hopper and Joyce question Jonathan at the police station, and Hopper overhears some key information that connects Eleven to the boys. Hopper, Joyce, Nancy and Jonathan go to the Byers house where they use Will's walkie-talkie to contact the kids. Steve has a crisis of conscience and seeks to make amends with Nancy. After a run-in with Hawkins National Laboratory agents, Hopper and the kids meet up with Joyce, Nancy and Jonathan at the Byers house. The group heads to Hawkins Middle School, where they set up a makeshift isolation tank so that Eleven can contact Will. Hopper and Joyce head to Hawkins National Laboratory in search of Will, while Nancy and Jonathan steal back their hunting gear from the police station and prepare to go monster hunting.

MONSTERS	✓	KISSING	✗
FLASHBACK	✓	TELEKINESIS	✓
NOSEBLEED	✓	BARB	✗

MUSICAL MOMENT

'Should I Stay Or Should I Go' by The Clash (again!) -- sung by a very sick-looking Will, all alone in the Upside Down.

TRIVIA

Getting Eleven to float in a kiddie pool wasn't a special effect: over 540 kilograms (1200 pounds) of Epsom salts were dissolved into the pool, making the water dense enough to float in.

MEMORABLE QUOTE

'Why are you keeping this curiosity door locked?'
-- Dustin Henderson

CHAPTER 8: THE UPSIDE DOWN

Caught sneaking into the Hawkins National Laboratory,
Hopper and Joyce are interrogated by Dr Brenner and his
men. Hopper cuts a deal. Nancy and Jonathan set a trap for
the monster inside the Byers house, only to have Steve show
up. The three of them join forces to fight the monster and
Steve, armed with a baseball bat, becomes an unlikely hero.
Back at Hawkins Middle School, Mike and Eleven share a moment
before they're rudely interrupted by Dr Brenner and his agents,
followed in quick succession by the monster. A battle ensues
and Eleven uses her powers to defeat the Demogorgon -- but at
great personal cost. Meanwhile, Joyce and Hopper enter the
Upside Down via the Lab and finally locate Will. Hopper
revives Will and the three of them escape together.

One month later: the four boys play *Dungeons & Dragons* in
Mike's basement; Nancy and Steve share a Christmas moment;
and Joyce, Jonathan and Will have been reunited. Hopper
leaves a box of Eggos in the woods. And stepping away from
his family dinner, Will coughs up a black slug, the lights
flicker and, for a moment, he's back in the Upside Down ...

MONSTERS	✓	KISSING	✓
FLASHBACK	✓	TELEKINESIS	✓
NOSEBLEED	✓	BARB	✗

MUSICAL MOMENT

'White Christmas' by Bing Crosby, a suitably festive and
comforting track playing as the Byers family sits down for
Christmas Eve dinner.

TRIVIA

The Demogorgon is considered the most powerful villain in
the first edition of *Advanced Dungeons & Dragons*, making its
debut in the 1976 supplementary rulebook *Eldritch Wizardry*.
The Demogorgon is known as the Prince of Demons.

MEMORABLE QUOTE

'Pudding? It's like this chocolate goo you eat with a spoon.'
-- Dustin Henderson

WILL

CHARACTER PROFILE:
WILL BYERS

Will Byers must be the unluckiest kid
in Hawkins. Snatched by a Demogorgon
on his way home from a Dungeons &
Dragons session with Mike, Dustin and
Lucas, Will emerged from his time in
the Upside Down suffering from PTSD and
experiencing terrifying visions (which
he dubbed 'now memories'). The son of
Lonnie and Joyce Byers, Will is a kind,
sensitive and creative boy who idolises
his older brother, Jonathan. Of all his
friends, he's closest to Mike, who he
met on the first day of kindergarten
-- 'I had no friends and I just felt
so alone and so scared, but I saw you
on the swings and you were alone, too,'
recalls Mike of their first meeting.
'You were just swinging by yourself.
And I just walked up to you and I
asked. I asked if you wanted to be my
friend. And you said yes. You said yes.
It was the best thing I've ever done.'

Hopper Cabin

Hawkins Police Station

Hopper Trailer

Melvald's General Store

Sinclair House

Wheeler House

Henderson House

Benny's Burgers

Hawkins High School

The Palace Arcade

Hawkins Middle School

Harrington House

Castle Byers

Byers House

Hawkins National Laboratory

Sattler Quarry

⋘ Hawkins ⋙

LOCATION GUIDE

Every place worth knowing about in Hawkins, Indiana.

Benny's Burgers

A home-style burger joint operated by Benny Hammond and located at 4819 Randolph Lane in Hawkins, Indiana. You'll find a jukebox playing the greatest hits from the '70s and life-affirming burgers and fries so good you'll want to steal them.

Byers house

A three-bedroom, single-storey house located in a heavily wooded part of Hawkins on the outskirts of town. Although not the fanciest of digs, it has a certain charm. If you can overlook the inter-dimensional portals, it's really quite homey! The Byers house is accessible via Mirkwood, but maybe don't take that route alone at night – who knows what could be lurking in the forest!

Castle Byers

A forest hideout built by Will and Jonathan Byers. All friends welcome, but you need to know the password to enter. (Just quietly, it's Radagast.)

The Gate

An inter-dimensional doorway located deep within the Hawkins National Laboratory. Eleven unintentionally created the Gate during an experiment run by Dr Brenner, allowing the creatures from the Upside Down to gain access to the human world.

Harrington house

A modern two-storey home, notable for its heated outdoor swimming pool. Located on one of Hawkins' nicer streets, the Harrington house is set against a heavily wooded area that's equally good at obscuring a teenager skulking around with a camera as it is hiding the approach of terrifying monsters from the Nether.

Hawk Cinema

Hawkins' beloved picture house. This is the place where Jonathan first experienced the thrill of *Evil Dead*, Dustin saw *Star Wars: Return of the Jedi* five times and Steve very publicly worked through some jealousy issues surrounding Nancy.

Hawkins High School

A public, co-ed high school located next to Hawkins Middle School. Like all high schools, it's characterised by cliques: from the cool kids like Steve, Tommy H and Carol, the studious types with their GPA averages of 3.999 (hello, Nancy and Barb) rebels like Billy, to outcasts and weirdos like Jonathan.

Hawkins Middle School

A place where all sorts of curiosity doors might be opened, thanks to the encouragement of teachers like Mr Clarke. Points of interest include the AV room (home to the Hawkins Middle AV Club), a cafeteria with a secret supply of Hunt's Snack Pack Chocolate Pudding, and an annual Snow Ball – an event anticipated with equal parts excitement and adolescent angst.

Hawkins National Laboratory

A national scientific research centre, which was established in the wake of World War II. Surrounded by barbed wire fences, under constant CCTV surveillance and guarded by armed military police, Hawkins National Laboratory is a division of the US Department of Energy. Since 1953, the Lab has been involved in experiments aimed at 'expanding the boundaries of the mind', as part of Project MKUltra. The Lab was run by Dr Martin Brenner until late 1983, after which Dr Sam Owens took over as Director of Operations.

Hawkins public library

Located in the centre of Hawkins town square, the library is the place you go when you're on a curiosity voyage and you need paddles ... which are books ... the books are the paddles.

Hawkins tunnel system

A mazelike, subterranean tunnel system located directly underneath the town of Hawkins. Spiralling out from the Gate within Hawkins National Laboratory, the tunnel system was created by the Mind Flayer as a way of infiltrating and infecting the human world. Will Byers was able to create a map of the Hawkins tunnel system while psychically linked to the Mind Flayer.

Henderson house

Home to Claudia, Dustin, Mews (and Tews) and Yertle, charmingly decorated in mid-century style.

Holland house

Currently for sale.

Hopper cabin

Originally built by Jim Hopper's grandfather, and located in a remote, wooded part of Hawkins. While this cabin really doesn't look like much from the outside, it's actually not a bad place to hide out when the government is looking for you.

Hopper trailer

A certified bachelor pad located by a lake. Watch out for the pesky bugs.

Junkyard

Need somewhere to abandon an old car or school bus? This is the spot. Doubles as a good place to hide from government agents, roaming Demo-dogs, and insecurities about your friends' loyalties.

Melvald's General Store

Located in downtown Hawkins, right next to Radio Shack. Melvald's takes its name from owner Donald Melvald and is Joyce Byers' place of employment. Known for its wide array of Christmas lights.

Mirkwood

A road located where Cornwallis and Kerley streets meet, in close proximity to the Byers house and the Harrington house. It takes its name from a great forest in a region of Tolkien's Middle-earth called Wilderland. The forest was originally known as Greenwood the Great, but after the shadow of the necromancer Sauron fell upon the forest, people began to call it Mirkwood. Hey, you asked!

The Palace Arcade

Hawkins' arcade, home to such classic games as *Dragon's Lair, Dig Dug, Centipede, Galaga* and *Pac-Man*, and a frequent hangout spot of Mike, Will, Dustin and Lucas.

Radio Shack

Hawkins' premier purveyor of audio-visual equipment. Radio Shack is located next door to Melvald's General Store and was Bob Newby's place of employment prior to his tragic death in 1984.

Sattler Quarry

A large, water-filled quarry, best known as the place where a body, initially believed to be Will Byers, was found. The quarry is 60 metres (200 feet) deep and jumping in it would likely result in instant death.

Sinclair house

A comfortable two-storey house located on Maple Street, not far from where the Wheelers live. Home to Lucas, Erica and Mr and Mrs Sinclair.

The Upside Down

An alternate dimension that is a nightmare reflection of our own. Home to the Mind Flayer, Demogorgons and many other things that will definitely try to kill you. Accessible via the Gate, various temporary portals or a deep psychic state.

Wheeler house

A large, four-bedroom house located on Maple Street, notable for its multi-purpose basement —the perfect place to host a 10-hour *Dungeons & Dragons* campaign, build a pillow fort or shelter the occasional runaway.

THE VOTES ARE IN!
CHIEF JIM HOPPER NAMED
HAWKINS' MOST ELIGIBLE BACHELOR

Hawkins is not short of single men, but a recent vote has determined which of our town's residents is setting the most hearts aflame. A light-hearted vote run by the Women of Hawkins Social Committee has determined that nothing beats a man in uniform: Police Chief Jim Hopper is this year's Most Eligible Bachelor!

The voters, who submitted their choice anonymously, cited the Chief's strong work ethic, sense of humour and hunky physique as just some of the many reasons why he should be voted Hawkins' most wanted. And of course it doesn't hurt that Hop knows how to handle himself in a dangerous situation.

Chief Hopper beat out Hawkins' High School English teacher Danny Davies, farmer Jack O'Dell and resident daredevil George Burness in this year's competition, with the Committee noting that although there were many strong entries, there was one clear winner. 'The Chief has it all,' said Committee member Bev Mooney. 'He's an upstanding member of the community, a credit to the Police Force and he sure does fill out that uniform nice. We're thrilled to name him this year's winner!'

When told about the news, Chief Hopper laughed for two minutes straight and then thanked the Social Committee for their endowment. 'I'm speechless,' said the Chief. 'Really.' Chief Hopper will be honoured with a framed certificate and a gift voucher to Hunting & Camping in downtown Hawkins.

The Women of Hawkins Social Committee would like to remind residents that they are running a white elephant sale in the Hawkins Middle School forecourt next Saturday to raise money for the Hawkins Cats & Dogs home. The sale will be on from 10 am until 4 pm, with a fry-up thanks to the folks at Bradley's Big Buy.

GET EL'S LOOK

PRETTY IN PINK

The dress may have been Nancy's, but Eleven makes it all her own. Part girly daydream, part practical disguise, this look takes Eleven's style from 'just escaped from the psych ward' to 'second cousin visiting from Sweden' in an instant.

In the words of a love-struck Mike Wheeler, she looks pretty ... uh, good. She looks pretty good.

THIS BLONDE FANTASY IS AS INEXPLICABLE AS IT IS BEAUTIFUL

JACKET IS A PRACTICAL TOUCH COURTESY OF MIKE'S CLOSET

PINK, GIRLY AND SWEET: THE PERFECT DISGUISE

STRIPED SOCKS OFFSET THE PRIM VIBE

GOOD FOR RUNNING AWAY FROM GOVERNMENT AGENTS

DUSTIN

CHARACTER PROFILE: DUSTIN HENDERSON

The beloved only child of Claudia Henderson and an absent father, Dustin is the most extroverted one in his circle of friends. Armed with a smart mouth, a deep love of science and a (nearly) unshakeable conviction of his own awesomeness, Dustin can always be relied on to use his nerd powers to come up with a crazy, yet somehow effective plan. He's an animal lover (who counts a cat, a turtle and a baby Demogorgon among his pets) and the kind of kid who always knows where the snacks are. Born with cleidocranial dysplasia, Dustin's acquisition of a set of pearly whites -- and a pep talk from his unlikely babysitter-turned-BFF Steve -- has seen his confidence boosted to even greater heights. And not even that cruel rejection from Stacey is going to bring him down.

What I Did On My Holidays
by Dustin Henderson

My Christmas holiday was one of the best and funnest of my life. I'll never forget what a great time I had with my friends. It was especially fun because we all thought Will was dead, but it turned out that it actually was some other kid. We still don't know who.

My favourite part of the holidays was hanging out with my best friends Mike, Lucas and Will and playing DUNGEONS & DRAGONS. My character is a bard. We played an awesome campaign and defeated the Thessalhydra, just like how we took down the bad men from the Lab and defeated the Demogorgon in real life. It was really fun but we all wished Eleven could have been there. Eleven is our mage. She can move things with her mind, and even flip over a van if she wants to. She's really weird, but I miss her.

Other than hanging out at Mike's place, I also spent a lot of time at the Palace playing DIG DUG. I'm definitely going to beat the high score soon.

In conclusion, it was a really fun holiday and I'm happy that Will is alive.

THE END

Dustin – very creative, but the assignment was to write an essay, not a work of fiction.

D+

Monster Manual

A guide to Hawkins' most terrifying

VINES

LARVAL DEMOGORGON

Although they resemble plants, these organisms from the Upside Down are part of the Mind Flayer's hive mind. These tendrils grow and wrap around surfaces like vines, possess rudimentary consciousness, and hiss and writhe like snakes. They are predators and seem to have a symbiotic relationship with the Demogorgons, trapping prey so that the monsters can feed on them. The vines may also produce the spores that are present in the atmosphere of the Upside Down, and their invasion into the human world has been known to poison crops and trees. Their only known weakness is fire.

In its nascent stage, the Demogorgon resembles a large, common garden slug. Slimy, dark greenish-brown and covered with bright yellow spots, these creepy-crawlies have a nasty habit of slithering down the throats of humans and making them into unwilling hosts – both Barb and Will were subjected to this parasitism, and for Barb (poor Barb!) it was fatal.

POLLYWOG DEMOGORGON

As the Demogorgon grows, it develops a pair of forelimbs with clawlike paws, a flexible tail and the tendency to make a purring, chittering sound. At this stage, it's actually kind of cute, resembling a terrestrial tadpole approximately the size of a mouse. Pollywogs have yellowish-green skin, are sensitive to both light and heat and have opportunistic eating habits: they will consume anything from household garbage to nougat.

QUADRUPED DEMOGORGON

JUVENILE DEMOGORGON

After the Demogorgon has consumed sufficient nutrients, it kicks into its next stage of evolution: the quadruped phase. At this point, the Demogorgon develops a pair of hind legs, becoming quadrupedal, and its skin-tone deepens to dark green. Its body mass increases, making it about the size of a guinea pig, and it develops small, sharp teeth.

During this stage the Demogorgon moults, shedding its skin to usher in a new, terrifying phase of development. It grows again, to about the size of a small dog. Its skin takes on a darker colour. It loses its sensitivity to light and gains its signature petal mouth, complete with row upon row of pointy teeth. Oh, and it becomes carnivorous. Around about now would be a good time to hide any pets you have, as they're likely to end up as the Demogorgon's dinner. (Has anybody seen Mews?)

DEMO-DOG

After moulting again, the Demogorgon reaches the penultimate stage of its life cycle: the Demo-dog phase. The adolescent Demogorgon develops in size, strength and intelligence. Its skin turns black and it grows to roughly the size of a large dog. It's now capable of killing and devouring a fully-grown human. They're fast and extremely strong, as well as cunning and agile, Demo-dogs can dig tunnels, climb steep precipices and work together to hunt and take down their prey. However, if you want to take *them* down, you better come armed with some serious fire power …

Mature Demogorgon

After moulting one more time, the Demogorgon reaches its final and most terrifying phase of development. It grows again, and acquires the ability to walk on two legs. Now standing at over 180 centimetres (6 feet), the Demogorgon is as tall as a human, and quite possibly smarter, possessing telekinetic abilities in addition to cold-blooded intelligence. With its immense strength, keen sense of smell and thick, nearly impenetrable skin, the Demogorgon is a fearsome hunter and nearly impossible to kill. A wrist-rocket is definitely not going to cut it – you're going to want someone with supernatural abilities to take down this one.

THE MIND FLAYER

Also known as the Shadow Monster, this powerful, malevolent entity has the ability to psychically control everything that resides in the Upside Down. As with the Demogorgon, the Mind Flayer takes its name from a *Dungeons & Dragons* baddie – in this case from a race of super-intelligent humanoids with octopus-like heads, who eat the brains of sentient beings and use their psionic abilities to psychically possess human hosts. Like its *D&D* counterpart, the

Mind Flayer is able to exert control over everything in the Upside Down as part of its hive mind, possess human hosts and even influence the atmosphere. While you can fight the Mind Flayer's possession of a human host by subjecting the infected body to high levels of heat, there's no known way to defeat it. The best you can hope for is to force it back to its own realm – and, even then, the Mind Flayer won't stay trapped for long …

LUCAS

CHARACTER PROFILE:
LUCAS SINCLAIR

Lucas is the voice of reason within his gang. He's smart, sceptical and independent, the kind of kid who wants to consider his options before rushing in. While his stubborn pragmatism sometimes rubs his more impulsive friends the wrong way, he's also the most perceptive and level-headed member of the group -- traits which have served him well, whether it comes to solving Hawkins National Lab-related mysteries or crushing on Max Mayfield. Lucas is the son of Mr and Mrs Sinclair, brother to sassiest-ever Erica and the only person in Hawkins who can wear a bandana and get away with it.

HEROIC GROWN-UPS

JOYCE BYERS

Joyce Byers is doing it tough – she's a single parent with a deadbeat ex and mind-numbing job. After her son Will goes missing, she's the first to cotton on to the fact that there are supernatural forces at play ... and she doesn't care how crazy it makes her look to tell people about them. Her love for her children is unshakeable, and when she sets her mind to something, you'd better not stand in her way. Joyce is quick-thinking, loving, compassionate, fierce and just trying to do the best she can for her kids with what she's got.

JIM HOPPER

After the tragic death of his daughter and subsequent collapse of his marriage, Hawkins Chief of Police Jim Hopper had fallen into a deep depression, abusing booze and prescription drugs just to get through the day. The vanishing of Will Byers forces him to drag himself out of that hole and back into life, where he proves to be loyal, brave and pretty damn good at his job. Becoming a de facto dad to Eleven opens some old wounds relating to the loss of his daughter, so he's sometimes unsuccessful at navigating this whole parenting thing – but he loves El and would do anything to protect her, even if it means being a little heavy-handed on the rules sometimes. Oh, and he totally has a thing for Joyce Byers. Just saying.

BOB NEWBY

Radio Shack employee, lover of Halloween, puzzle enthusiast, massive nerd, perfect boyfriend, heartbreaking hero and human ray of sunshine. As a relatively new beau of Joyce, Bob was a hundred per cent there for the Byers family. When Bob eventually discovers the real reason for Will's unusual behaviour, he's quick to use his big brain and even bigger heart to figure out that Will's drawings are, in fact, a giant map of Hawkins. Proving himself to be a better kind of human than most, Bob sacrifices himself to save Joyce, Mike and Hopper from the Demodogs that invade the Hawkins Lab. We miss you, Bob. This world did not deserve you.

SCOTT CLARKE

Mr Clarke is the science teacher at Hawkins Middle School – the kind of truly inspiring teacher you look back on fondly for the rest of your life. He's brilliant at explaining complex theoretical science, treats his students as intellectual equals, and would never dream of keeping a curiosity door locked. Mr Clarke also runs the Middle AV Club, allowing the kids access to the Heathkit ham shack they use to contact Will in the Upside Down. He rocks a moustache and sweater vest like no one else and always has the perfect metaphor to make even the most arcane scientific theory make sense.

BENNY HAMMOND

Proprietor of Benny's Burgers, the gruff Benny Hammond is probably the first person to ever show Eleven real kindness. Benny is able to coax El into trusting him enough to give her a change of clothes and some food. In a misguided attempt to help her, Benny calls what he thinks is social services, only to become the latest victim of Hawkins National Laboratory's shady and highly illegal practices.

MURRAY BAUMAN

A private investigator hired by the Holland family to investigate Barb's disappearance, Murray Bauman's eccentricities and penchant for wild conspiracies clearly hampered his career as an investigative journalist at the *Chicago Sun-Times*. While Bauman is something of a crackpot, he helps Nancy and Jonathan figure out a way to expose Hawkins National Laboratory – and FINALLY get justice for Barb – by using his cynical worldview and grasp of media manipulation to its full advantage. He also loves to meddle in the love lives of the people around him, perhaps to make up for the loneliness of his own existence.

DR SAM OWENS

Taking over from Dr Brenner as Director of Operations at Hawkins Lab, Dr Owens isn't, at first glance, a very likeable guy. While he appears kindly in his treatment of Will Byers, it's clear he has his own agenda relating to his research into the Upside Down. Ultimately, though, Dr Owens comes through, risking his own life to help Joyce, Hopper and Mike escape from the Demo-dog-infested Hawkins Lab. He also acquires a forged birth certificate for Eleven, making her legally Hopper's daughter and allowing her to go by the less numerically-minded name Jane Hopper.

RADIO SHACK
INTERNAL MEMO

30 September 1984

Attn: all staff

Hello folks, and thank you all for another great year at Radio Shack. You'll be pleased to know that we've ended the fiscal year on a high note, with sales up year-on-year across the majority of our stores.

Now it's my great pleasure to announce our Employee of the Year: Hawkins' Radio Shack manager Bob Newby! Since his promotion to manager, Bob has shown true leadership, consistently hitting his sales targets and guiding the store to a very profitable fourth quarter. But it's not just the bottom line that we care about here at Radio Shack: we want to give our customers the best possible experience in store every time. I was pleased to receive this note from a Hawkins resident, which read:

Thank you to your staff member Bob Newby for his superlative service. I'm a regular at Radio Shack (my latest purchase was a Heathkit ham shack radio -- phenomenal!), and every time I visit, Bob is only too happy to give me recommendations on VHS versus Betamax or walk me through what the TRS-80 Model 4 personal computer can do. It's a genuine pleasure to encounter someone who's so passionate about their job. He's a credit to the Radio Shack team!

Please join me in congratulating our 1984 Radio Shack Employee of the Year!

R. Morgan

VP OF RADIO SHACK

⇒ The ⇐

UPSIDE DOWN

'... a dimension that is a dark reflection, or echo, of our world. It is a place of decay and death, a plane out of phase, a place of monsters. It is right next to you and you don't even see it ...'

— *Advanced Dungeons & Dragons Expert Rulebook*

Also known as:

The Nether, The Vale of Shadows.

What is the Upside Down?

The Upside Down is an alternate dimension that exists parallel to our world. Imagine a *Dungeons & Dragons* board on which you map out your campaign: our world is everything that exists on top of the board. Flip the board over. That's the Upside Down – like our world but cold, dark and empty of human life. Obscured by ever-present mist, overrun by grasping tendrils and populated by vicious monsters, the Upside Down is a hellish nightmare-scape from which few make it out.

What lives there?

The Upside Down is home to a variety of life-forms, none of them human.

There are semi-sentient vines that will slither out of the ground and wrap themselves around you so you can't escape. The air is hazy with spores that will make you sick if you breathe them in for too long. There are hyper-intelligent predators that grow from sluglike larvae, to ferocious mutant canines and full-blown humanoid monsters. Most terrifying of all is a gargantuan, multi-limbed monster known as the Mind Flayer – a creature able to telepathically control everything that resides in the Upside Down and even exert its will on human minds.

Where did it come from?

Nobody knows. First contact was made with the Upside Down in November 1983, during an experiment at Hawkins National Laboratory designed to use Eleven's psychic abilities to listen into Russian intelligence. During the experiment, Eleven encountered a growling sound, which was broadcast back to the scientists at the Lab. Dr Brenner then set up an experiment to discover more about the creature and sent Eleven to make contact. In the moment contact was established, a fissure between the two dimensions was created, which allowed the monster, and other horrors from the Upside Down, to gain access to our world.

How do you get there?

First up, it's certainly not advisable to enter the Upside Down (seriously – you remember what happened to Barb, right?). But if you really have to venture into the Vale of Shadows to rescue a friend, it's not going to be easy. As Mr Clarke explains, think of our dimension like a tightrope, on which stands an acrobat (in this metaphor, think of yourself as the acrobat). The acrobat can move forwards or backwards along the rope. But next to the acrobat is a flea. The flea can also travel back and forth, but it can also travel along the side of the rope and even go underneath the rope – in other words, it can go upside down. The only way the acrobat can go upside down is to create a massive amount of energy to open up a tear in time and space so large that it smashes through to the alternate dimension, thereby creating a doorway. Sound familiar? Hawkins is home to the Hawkins Power and Light plant, a source of a massive amount of energy. And Eleven is in possession of extraordinary psychic abilities, which she can use to manipulate energy in violent ways – maybe even enough to punch a hole in time and space. But it's not only Eleven who can create inter-dimensional rifts. The Demogorgon, using its psychic abilities, is also able to create both large rifts and smaller tears. These portals don't last forever, but while they're open, both humans and monsters can pass freely between the two worlds.

What is the Gate?

The Gate is the primary portal to the Upside Down. Unlike the temporary portals created by the Demogorgon, the Gate didn't close up on its own, enabling the darkness from the Upside Down to seep into our world. Also known as the Rift, the Gate is located in the underground subsystem of Hawkins National Laboratory, and its power is so strong that it can disrupt the local electromagnetic field, causing compasses to point towards it instead of true north. The Gate has the capacity to grow larger over time, suggesting that if it were not closed, it would eventually envelop the whole of our world.

STEVE

CHARACTER PROFILE:
STEVE HARRINGTON

Steve 'The King' Harrington. Steve 'The Hair' Harrington. Steve 'Like a Ninja' Harrington. Once a known player and ringleader of Hawkins' coolest clique, Steve turned over a new leaf when he started dating Nancy (and was unwittingly exposed to Demogorgons, telekinesis and the Upside Down -- hey, it's bound to change your perspective on things). Maybe he's not the sharpest crayon in the box, but Steve has a good heart (and a way with a studded baseball bat). He genuinely wants the best for Nancy. He's big enough to admit when he's acted stupidly and he's willing to risk his life for his girlfriend's little brother's friends. We like Steve, but we don't love Steve. No, wait -- we definitely do.

STEVE HARRINGTON'S TOP SECRET GUIDE TO PERFECT HAIR

ALTHOUGH THE KEY TO GIRLS IS ACTING LIKE YOU DON'T CARE, HAVING A REALLY GREAT HAIRDO CERTAINLY HELPS. CHANNEL A LITTLE OF THE KING'S MAGIC WITH THIS STEP-BY-STEP GUIDE TO ACHIEVING MULLET MAGIC.

STEP 1

Wash your hair using
Fabergé Organics. Use
the shampoo AND
conditioner.

STEP 2

When your hair is damp — it's not wet,
okay? — when it's DAMP, do four puffs
of the Farrah Fawcett spray. Note:
the full name is 'Farrah Fawcett Hair
Spray with Vitamins and Minerals' (also
by Fabergé), and you can choose from
'Regular Hold' or 'For Hard to Hold Hair'.

STEP 3

Flip your head over and blow-dry the
heck out of your hair to get the volume
happening. Then blow-dry the sides back,
blow-dry it up in the back to show off
the mullet and then blow-dry a few
pieces down in the front.

STEP 4

Run your fingers through
your hair to tousle it
up. Yep, you are looking
majestic.

STEP 5

Tell no one your secret. Seriously, you
tell anyone I just told you that, and your
ass is grass. You're dead, Henderson.

GET EL'S LOOK

CABIN FEVER

Hopper may be a great dad, but when it comes to dressing his adopted daughter, he's kinda sorta clueless. It's like he just went to the thrift store and bought the first thing he saw that looked vaguely the right size. Still, when you've been stuck in a cabin for 353 days, fashion isn't going to be high on your priority list – not when the bad men are still out there looking for you ...

HAIR
IS WILD,
UNTAMED,
FREE

JACKET IS
SEVERAL
SIZES TOO
LARGE

OVERALLS ARE
PRACTICAL
BUT CUTE

STILL GOOD
FOR RUNNING
AWAY FROM
GOVERNMENT
AGENTS

CHAPTER 1: MADMAX

28 October 1984: a mysterious girl named Kali is
involved in a high-speed chase with the police but,
after demonstrating supernatural powers, she escapes.
Meanwhile in Hawkins, Will experiences increasingly
disturbing flashbacks to the Upside Down. Hopper
investigates a biological anomaly, which is destroying
local crops. The boys meet a new gamer in town -- a girl
named Maxine Mayfield, who's just moved to Hawkins with
her stepbrother Billy Hargrove. Nancy struggles with her
guilt over Barb's death. Joyce spends time with her new
boyfriend, Bob Newby. Hopper travels to his cabin in
the woods, where it's revealed he's been hiding Eleven
for 352 days.

MONSTERS	✓	KISSING	✓
FLASHBACK	✓	TELEKINESIS	✓
NOSEBLEED	✗	BOB	✓

MUSICAL MOMENT

'Rock You Like a Hurricane' by Scorpions, when, to the
visible approval of the female cohort, Billy makes his
grand entrance to Hawkins High School.

TRIVIA

In the initial character notes, Kali was billed as
a character named Roman and described as 'a male or a
female of any ethnicity between the ages of 30 and 38'.

MEMORABLE QUOTE

'It's finger-lickin' good.' -- Steve Harrington

CHAPTER 2: TRICK OR TREAT, FREAK

Hopper and Eleven disagree about her confinement. Mike, Will, Dustin and Lucas invite Max to go trick-or-treating with them, while Nancy and Steve attend a Halloween party. Nancy gets drunk and tells Steve that she doesn't love him, and Jonathan is the one who ends up taking her home. Will's visions of the Upside Down get worse. Eleven attempts to use her psychic abilities to contact Mike but isn't successful. Meanwhile, Dustin discovers something mysterious in his garbage bin ...

MONSTERS	✓	KISSING	✓
FLASHBACK	✓	TELEKINESIS	✓
NOSEBLEED		BOB	✓

MUSICAL MOMENT

'Girls On Film' by Duran Duran, playing as Jonathan arrives at the Halloween party (a subtle nod to his voyeuristic habits).

TRIVIA

For the Halloween party, Steve and Nancy are dressed up as Joel (Tom Cruise) and Lana (Rebecca De Mornay) from *Risky Business* (1983).

MEMORABLE QUOTE

'I hope it doesn't suck!' -- Bob Newby

CHAPTER 3: THE POLLYWOG

Dustin adopts the mysterious creature he found in his garbage bin and names it D'Artagnan, or Dart for short. Bob advises Will to confront his fears. Nancy and Jonathan resolve to tell Barb's parents the truth about her disappearance. Dustin brings a rapidly growing Dart to school, only to have him escape. After growing impatient with her captivity and Hopper's 'Don't be stupid' rules, Eleven leaves the cabin to look for Mike. Taking Bob's advice, Will confronts the terrifying Shadow Monster from his visions, with disastrous results.

MONSTERS	✓	KISSING	✗
FLASHBACK	✓	TELEKINESIS	✓
NOSEBLEED	✗	BOB	✓

MUSICAL MOMENT

'You Don't Mess Around With Jim' by Jim Croce, playing as Hopper does the ultimate dad dance for Eleven.

TRIVIA

According to Eleven, she hasn't seen Mike for 326 days. Hold up: 3 + 2 + 6 = 11. Well played, Duffer Brothers. Well played.

MEMORABLE QUOTE

'However I am on a curiosity voyage, and I need my paddles to travel. These books -- these books are my paddles.'
-- Dustin Henderson

CHAPTER 4: WILL THE WISE

Dustin, Mike, Lucas, Max and Joyce find Will almost
catatonic after being possessed by the Shadow Monster.
Eleven returns home to a furious Hopper and, when she
is grounded, throws a tantrum, and uses her telekinetic
abilities to violent effect. Nancy and Jonathan's mission
to talk to Barb's parents is intercepted by government
agents, and they're taken to Hawkins Lab where Dr Owens
shows them the Gate to the Upside Down. Nancy records
the entire exchange with the intention of exposing the
truth. Will begins to draw out his visions, leading Hopper
to a discovery. After finding out information about her
past, Eleven makes psychic contact with her mother, Terry
Ives. Dustin returns home to find that Dart has grown
significantly, escaped his cage and eaten the family cat.
Out in the field, Hopper discovers a massive network of
tunnels, full of rot from the Upside Down.

MONSTERS	✓	KISSING	✓
FLASHBACK	✓	TELEKINESIS	✓
NOSEBLEED	✓	BOB	✓

MUSICAL MOMENT

'This Is Radio Clash' by the Clash, an appropriately
rebellious song that plays while Nancy tells her mother
she's going to have a 'girls' night' when she's really
going to meet Jonathan

TRIVIA

Will's drawings were actually masterminded and created by
Stranger Things prop master Lynda Reiss and her team -- it
took them four months to create over 3000 illustrations,
and used 1500 Crayola crayons.

MEMORABLE QUOTE

'Let's burn that Lab to the ground.' -- Nancy Wheeler

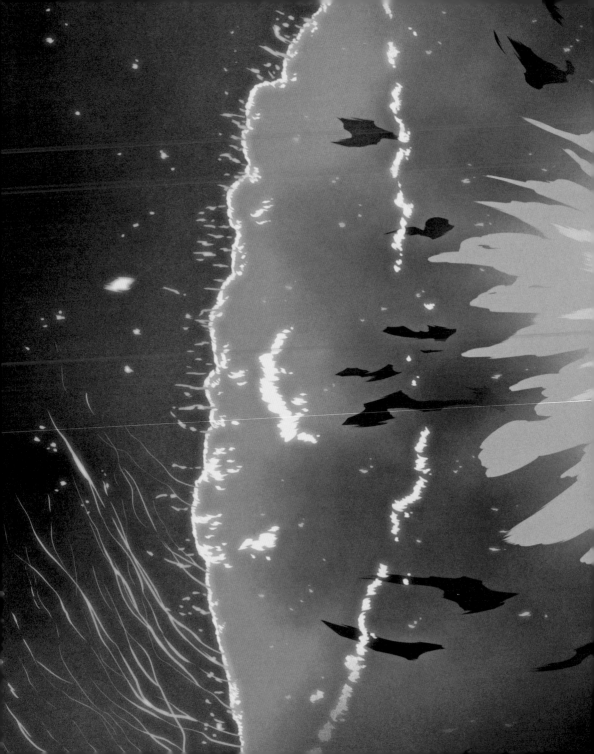

CHAPTER 5: DIG DUG

In the tunnels, Hopper is overcome by the poisonous spores of the Upside Down and loses consciousness. Will confesses to Mike that he feels connected to the Shadow Monster and then demonstrates that connection when he realises that Hopper is in danger. Eleven hitchhikes to her mother's house but finds her stuck in a fugue state -- but, in a vision, she encounters a girl who shares her psychic gifts. Jonathan and Nancy seek out Murray Bauman and come up with a plan to expose the Hawkins National Laboratory's secrets. Bob realises that Will's drawings are actually a map of Hawkins and launches a mission to find Hopper. Dustin teams up with Steve to deal with Dart. Joyce, Bob, Will and Mike locate Hopper and, with the help of flamethrower-wielding technicians from Hawkins National Laboratory, manage to rescue him from being consumed by the Upside Down's vines. But it's not just the vines that are burning up ...

MONSTERS	✓	KISSING	✗
FLASHBACK	✓	TELEKINESIS	✓
NOSEBLEED	✗	BOB	✓

MUSICAL MOMENT

'No More' by Billie Holiday, playing while Jonathan and Nancy divulge what they know to Bauman. And with lyrics like 'She tells her side, nothing to hide/Now the world will know just what the blues is all about', it couldn't be more appropriate.

TRIVIA

This episode takes its title from the classic 1982 arcade game *Dig Dug*, in which you play a character who digs underground tunnels where you must fight and defeat monsters.

MEMORABLE QUOTE

'Sorry but you ate my cat!' -- Dustin Henderson

CHAPTER 6: THE SPY

Will is rushed to the infirmary at Hawkins National Laboratory as Joyce becomes increasingly frantic. Dustin and Steve discover that Dart has grown again -- and is on the loose. Nancy, Jonathan and Bauman set a plan in motion to expose Hawkins Lab's culpability in Barb's death. Nancy and Jonathan spend the night together. Back at the Lab, Will wakes up but isn't acting like himself. Dr Owens realises that Will is connected to the Shadow Monster's hive mind virus. Lucas gets Max up to speed on everything the gang has experienced, and they head out to meet Steve and Dustin, who have laid a trap to capture Dart. Will uses his psychic link to the Shadow Monster to reveal where it's hiding, and the scientists send technicians to investigate. While Hopper and Dr Owens watch from the control room, Will tells Mike and Joyce that the Shadow Monster coerced him into giving false information: it's a trap. Meanwhile, Steve, Dustin, Lucas and Max have their own problems at the junkyard, which has been overrun by a pack of Demo-dogs. They take shelter in an abandoned bus, when suddenly the Demo-dogs leave -- they've been called away by the hive mind and head to the tunnels where they make quick, bloody work of the technicians. In the control room, Hopper and Dr Owens watch in horror as the Demo-dogs rise up from the tunnels and make their way into the Lab ...

MONSTERS	✓	KISSING	✓
FLASHBACK	✗	TELEKINESIS	✓
NOSEBLEED	✗	BOB	✓

MUSICAL MOMENT

'Round And Round' by Ratt, playing as Billy is lifting weights and generally being the most '80s guy.

TRIVIA

This is the only episode in which Eleven does not appear.

MEMORABLE QUOTE

'Bunch of nerds.' -- Erica Sinclair

CHAPTER 7: THE LOST SISTER

After gleaning information from Terry and Becky Ives, Eleven leaves Hawkins and heads to Chicago to track down the girl she saw in her vision. Now alone in an unfamiliar city, she comes across a warehouse where she meets a hostile crew of misfits: Axel, Funshine, Dottie, Mick and Kali. When Eleven demonstrates her telekinetic abilities, Kali reveals the number 008 tattooed on her arm. She's the girl Eleven saw in her psychic vision, another of Dr Brenner's experiments from the Lab. She shares Eleven's supernatural abilities -- except her power is to create illusions in people's minds that they believe are real. Kali helps Eleven hone her powers and then recruits her into her mission to wreak vengeance on the employees of Hawkins National Laboratory, who hurt them both. After giving Eleven a punk makeover, the crew head out to find the Hawkins Lab tech who put Eleven's mother in her vegetative state. Kali encourages Eleven to kill him, but she won't do it. After heading back to the warehouse, Kali asks Eleven to help her track down Dr Brenner to get justice for the pain he caused them both. Eleven uses her abilities to check in on Mike and Hopper and realises that they're in trouble. The police storm the warehouse, forcing Kali's crew to make a run for it. Kali asks Eleven to come with them, but she opts to return home to Hawkins to save her friends.

MONSTERS	✕	KISSING	✕
FLASHBACK	✓	TELEKINESIS	✓
NOSEBLEED	✓	BOB	✕

MUSICAL MOMENT

'Runaway' by Bon Jovi, an extremely literal choice playing as Eleven leaves Hawkins for Chicago.

TRIVIA

Eleven's punk makeover was partially inspired by Madonna, whose signature look in the '80s was to don an oversized power blazer, rolling up the sleeves and popping the collar.

MEMORABLE QUOTE

'Bitchin.' -- Eleven

CHAPTER 8: THE MIND FLAYER

As the Demo-dogs invade the Lab, Joyce sedates Will so that the Shadow Monster can't use him to spy on them. Bob volunteers to reboot the security system so that they can escape the now locked-down building. Dustin, Steve, Lucas and Max track the Demo-dogs to the Lab, where they meet up with Nancy and Jonathan. Bob manages to restore the systems, allowing Hopper, Will, Mike and Joyce to escape. As Bob is about to join them, he's brutally killed by a Demo-dog. Hopper, Joyce, Mike and Will join the rest of the crew, and they regroup at the Byers house. Dustin suggests that Will might be possessed by something akin to a Mind Flayer, a monster from *Dungeons & Dragons* mythology. As they interrogate Will, he taps out a message in morse code, instructing them to 'close gate'. But it's not long before the Mind Flayer figures out where they're hiding and sends the Demo-dogs to the house. But before they can attack, Eleven shows up and uses her powers to save her friends. The team is finally back together.

MONSTERS	✓	KISSING	✗
FLASHBACK	✗	TELEKINESIS	✓
NOSEBLEED	✓	BOB	✓

MUSICAL MOMENT

'Should I Stay Or Should I Go' by The Clash -- this time, Jonathan uses it as a way to reach out to Will through the Mind Flayer's influence.

TRIVIA

Bob Newby was originally going to be killed off in episode three, but the Duffer Brothers loved working with Sean Astin so much that they opted to keep him around right up to the penultimate episode.

MEMORABLE QUOTE

'Demogorgon dogs. Demo-dogs. It's like a compound. It's like a play on words, okay?' -- Dustin Henderson

CHAPTER 9: THE GATE

Eleven and Mike have an emotional reunion. The gang devises a plan to close the Gate and save Will from the Mind Flayer's influence. Eleven and Hopper head to the Lab. Billy arrives at the Byers house looking for Max -- he and Steve brawl before Max sedates her stepbrother with a hypodermic needle. Dustin, Lucas, Mike and Max head to the tunnels with an unconscious Steve in tow. When they arrive, they begin burning the vines so the Demo-dogs will flock to the tunnels and give Hopper and Eleven a chance to close the Gate. Hopper and Eleven reach the Lab to find everyone except Dr Owens dead. Joyce, Jonathan and Nancy expose Will to extreme heat in order to flush out the Mind Flayer. Finally, he wakes up as Will again, freed from the last of the Mind Flayer's influence. Hopper and Eleven reach the Gate, and when Eleven begins to telekinetically close it, the Mind Flayer senses her powers and re-routes the Demo-dogs to attack them. While Hopper fights off the Demo-dogs, Eleven channels all her strength to close the portal to the Upside Down, killing all the remaining Demogorgons in the process.

One month later: after Nancy and Jonathan's whistleblowing, the Hawkins National Laboratory is being shut down. Barb finally gets a funeral. Hopper meets with Dr Owens who gives him a forged birth certificate for Eleven: now she is legally Hopper's daughter. Joyce mourns Bob. Later, it's the Snow Ball. Lucas dances with Max, Dustin fails to impress the girls in his grade but scores a dance with Nancy, and Eleven shows up to share a dance with Mike. Meanwhile, in the Upside Down, the Mind Flayer looms over the school. Perhaps everything is not as safe as it seems ...

MONSTERS	✓	KISSING	✓
FLASHBACK	✓	TELEKINESIS	✓
NOSEBLEED	✓	BOB	✗

MUSICAL MOMENT

'Every Breath You Take' by The Police, playing as Mike and Eleven share their first kiss.

TRIVIA

The blue bracelet that Eleven wears at the Snow Ball is the one Hopper has worn since his daughter Sara died. It was originally Sara's hairband, which she can be seen wearing in flashbacks.

MEMORABLE QUOTE

'I may be a pretty shitty boyfriend, but turns out I'm actually a pretty damn good babysitter.' -- Steve Harrington

LOST CAT

HAVE YOU SEEN ME?
REWARD OFFERED

Answers to Mews. Last seen on 31 October near Loch Nora in Hawkins. Please contact Claudia Henderson if you have any information. Beloved pet, much missed.

NANCY

CHARACTER PROFILE:
NANCY WHEELER

Don't let those prim sweaters fool you
-- Nancy Wheeler is kind of a badass.
Daughter of Ted and Karen Wheeler and
sister to Mike and Holly, Nancy's
rebellions escalated from sneaking her
boyfriend Steve into her room for a
clandestine study session to arming
herself with a gun and going monster
hunting, and orchestrating an exposé
on Hawkins National Laboratory's
illegal activities. While she can be
occasionally self-centred (see: being
too busy getting fresh with Steve to
notice her friend Barbara's abduction
by Demogorgon), she's ultimately the
kind of person who'd do whatever it
takes to protect the ones she loves.
Speaking of which, will she end up
with clean-cut Steve, or embrace the
strange with Jonathan? Only time
will tell.

CHARACTER GUIDE:
EXTENDED FAMILIES

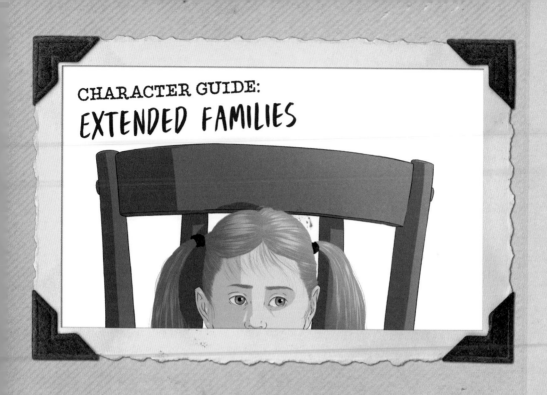

TED, KAREN & HOLLY WHEELER

The Wheelers are a 'perfect' nuclear family, living the American dream. They own a nice house. They can afford nice things. Karen Wheeler is a loving, although somewhat overbearing, mother stuck in a frustrating marriage (and all too easily sucked in by the dubious charms of Billy Hargrove). Ted Wheeler is not only a human black hole, devoid of any personality and completely oblivious to the strange events occurring right in front of him, he cluelessly goes along with Dr Brenner's questioning, telling Karen, 'Honey, we have to trust them, ok? This is our government, they're on our side.' Despite her youth and limited vocabulary, Holly Wheeler is enormously charismatic and clearly has all the personality that Ted is missing.

MR, MRS & ERICA SINCLAIR

Lucas' dad is a Vietnam vet who knows how to maintain a happy marriage. ('First, I apologise. Then I get your mother whatever she wants.' 'Even when she's wrong?' 'She's never wrong, son.') Mrs Sinclair adores her kids (and has a particular fondness for Ghostbuster costumes). The real hero of the Sinclair family is Erica, who has no bones calling her older brother out as a massive nerd, using his He-Man figurine to make out with her Barbie and eating all the damn syrup she wants.

MR, MRS & MEWS HENDERSON

Claudia Henderson is a loving and perceptive – if gullible – mother with a few boundary issues ('Are you constipated again?'). The void left by the apparent constant absence of Mr Henderson is filled by her deep devotion to Mews, a relatively unfriendly cat who meets his gory end as Dart's dinner.

MR & MRS HOLLAND

Kindly, loving parents of Barb. After the tragic disappearance of their daughter, the Hollands mortgage their house in order to hire private investigator (and conspiracy theorist) Murray Bauman. The true nature of Barb's death was deemed too much for the Hollands to cope with, so Nancy, Jonathan and Bauman concoct a more 'believable' death involving a chemical leak at the Lab, in order to give the Hollands the closure they so desperately need.

NEIL & SUSAN HARGROVE

Neil Hargrove is Billy Hargrove's biological father, recently married to Susan Hargrove (nee Mayfield), biological mother of Max Mayfield. Susan seems to be a relatively kind mother and stepmother, but does nothing to intervene in Neil's abusive behaviour towards Billy. Home life at the Hargrove house is bleak.

TERRY & BECKY IVES

Terry Ives is the mother of Eleven – or Jane, as she was originally named. Terry fought to rescue the daughter she knew had been kidnapped by Dr Martin Brenner following her involvement in Project MKUltra, an experiment that exposed her to mind-altering drugs. Brenner electrocuted Terry and trapped her in a vegetative state. Becky is Terry's carer, who clearly thinks her sister's belief that her child is not only alive but has psychic powers, are just the ravings of a madwoman who has done waaaaaay too much LSD.

DIANE & SARA HOPPER

Diane was married to Jim Hopper for seven years but they separated after their young daughter Sara's tragic death due to cancer. Diane is now married to Bill, with whom she has a baby.

LONNIE BYERS & CYNTHIA

Lonnie is the archetypal deadbeat dad to Jonathan and Will Byers. After Lonnie and Joyce divorced, Lonnie moved to Indianapolis, where he lives with his unsympathetic (and somewhat inappropriate) girlfriend, Cynthia.

AXEL, DOTTIE, MICK & FUNSHINE

The adopted family of Kali Prasad (aka Eight). The gang reside in an abandoned warehouse in Chicago, but live a nomadic life seeking vengeance on those who have hurt them in the past. Axel is an intimidating mohawked punk and 'spider hater', Dottie is the newest recruit to the gang, Mick is the 'eyes' of the group and Funshine is the burly 'warrior' who, despite his size, is actually a teddy bear.

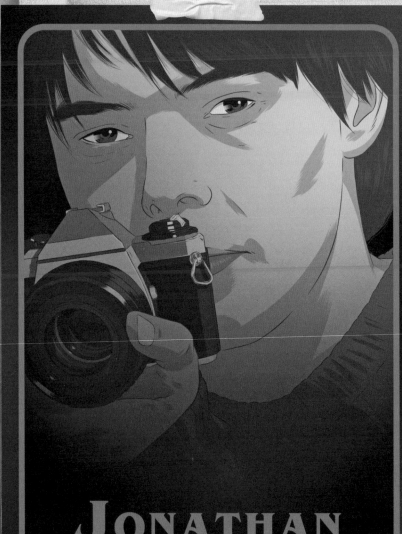

JONATHAN

CHARACTER PROFILE: JONATHAN BYERS

He reads Kurt Vonnegut. He listens to
Joy Division. He wouldn't be seen dead
at a party. Jonathan is your classic
moody teenager with a kind of creepy
habit of taking photos of people
without their knowledge. The child
of a broken home, Jonathan wears his
angst on his sleeve, making a point
of not caring if people think he's
a freak or a weirdo ('Nobody normal
ever accomplished anything meaningful
in this world,' he says). Jonathan
loves his little brother, Will, and
is fiercely protective of his mother,
Joyce -- even when he thinks she's
losing the plot.

HOPPER'S
'DON'T BE STUPID'
RULES

RULE NUMBER ONE
Always keep the curtains drawn.

RULE NUMBER TWO
Only open the door if you hear my secret knock.

RULE NUMBER THREE
Don't ever go out alone, especially not in the daylight.

SIDE A:

Black Sabbath – 'Symptom of the Universe' (6:29)

Scorpions – 'Rock You Like a Hurricane' (4:11)

Savage – 'Let It Loose' (3:21)

Van Halen – 'Girl Gone Bad' (4:35)

Billy Squier – 'The Stroke' (3:38)

Ted Nugent – 'Wango Tango' (4.50)

SIDE B:

Mötley Crüe – 'Shout at the Devil' (3:43)

Channel 3 – 'Strength in Numbers' (1:25)

Quiet Riot – 'Cum On Feel the Noize' (5.06)

Ratt – 'Round and Round' (4:24)

Night Ranger – 'Don't Tell Me You Love Me' (4.23)

Metallica – 'The Four Horsemen' (7:13)

QUIZ: WHAT'S YOUR DUNGEONS & DRAGONS CHARACTER CLASS?

You've been following this weird tunnel for a while. Strange vines cover every surface and a thick miasma fills the air. Heroes, it's time to gather around your Dungeon Master and toss a many-sided dice. Who should you play as, when you enter the world of Advanced *Dungeons & Dragons?*

A MONSTER APPEARS AND CHALLENGES YOU. YOU:

a) Try to appeal to its sense of reason

b) Try to appeal to its sense of goodness

c) Defend yourself from afar

d) Use your wiles to defuse the situation

e) Use magic to immobilise it

f) Outrun it

WHAT ARE YOU SEARCHING FOR?

a) Justice

b) A higher power

c) Independence

d) Knowledge

e) Magic

f) Speed

PICK AN OBJECT:

a) A shield

b) A holy book

c) A longbow

d) A lute

e) A spellbook

f) A skateboard

THE TRAITS THAT DEFINE YOU ARE:

a) Strength and charisma

b) Wisdom

c) Dexterity and wisdom

d) Charisma

e) Intelligence

f) Dexterity and speed

CHOOSE A MISSION:

a) Rescue a proud princess who's been unfairly imprisoned and restore her to her rightful place on the throne

b) Journey to a sept set high in the mountains to receive guidance and knowledge from the monks who reside there

c) Travelling solo, track down a monster that's been terrorising a village and kill it with a single shot from your longbow

d) Infiltrate an enemy court using only your wiles, charm them into divulging all their secrets and escape into the night before they realise what you've done

e) Fight off a horde of enemies using the power of your mind

f) Travel cross-country on a mission to acquire knowledge, experience and treasure

YOUR GREATEST FEAR IS:

a) Being betrayed by the people you love

b) Losing your faith

c) Losing your independence

d) Being at a loss for words

e) Losing your sense of wonder

f) Getting caught

CHOOSE YOUR EQUIPMENT:

a) A sword, a shield and a holy symbol

b) A staff, a shield and light armour

c) A longbow, a short sword and leather armour

d) A rapier, a musical instrument and light armour

e) A staff, a spellbook and a dagger

f) A dagger, a dart and light armour

A NECROMANCER OFFERS YOU A LARGE SUM OF MONEY IF YOU'LL HELP HER STEAL A LEGENDARY JEWEL THAT WILL INCREASE HER POWERS. YOU:

a) Decline because necromancy is morally wrong

b) Decline because necromancy is an affront to God

c) Accept as long as the price is right

d) Accept out of curiosity

e) Decline but go hunting for the jewel yourself

f) Accept with the intention of stealing the jewel once you've found it

CHOOSE YOUR SKILLS:

a) Intimidation and persuasion

b) Arcana and insight

c) Investigation and stealth

d) Performance and persuasion

e) Arcana and investigation

f) Investigation and deception

PICK AN APHORISM:

a) I serve

b) I believe

c) I seek

d) I imagine

e) I conjure

f) I journey

Mostly As: Paladin

Governed by a strong sense of morality and the urge to do what's right, your *Dungeons & Dragons* character should be a Paladin – just like Mike Wheeler. You are 'a holy warrior bound to a sacred oath', who doesn't hesitate to risk your own safety to protect the people you love. You value loyalty, compassion, honour and, above all, honesty: remember, *friends don't lie*.

Mostly Bs: Cleric

Like Will Byers, you should play as a Cleric: 'a priestly champion who wields divine magic in service of a higher power'. Clerics have big goals and wield big weapons. Chosen agents of the gods, they're conduits for divine power, manifesting supernatural abilities beyond the human realm. Sometimes Clerics are linked to merciful gods and sometimes to vengeful ones – but however you choose to play it, you're going to be in for a wild ride.

Cleric

Paladin

Mostly Cs: *Ranger*

Rangers are tactically-minded players who excel at stealth, reconnaissance and fighting from a distance. Described as 'a warrior who uses martial prowess and nature magic to combat threats on the edges of civilisation', Rangers are naturally suspicious – just like Lucas Sinclair – because they know that running headlong into unfamiliar territory will likely get you killed. You're pragmatic, level-headed and a natural explorer.

Mostly Ds: *Bard*

You're born to be a Bard, 'an inspiring magician whose power echoes the music of creation'. This is Dustin Henderson's choice of character class and, like Dustin, you're the kind of person who excels at talking your way out of problems rather than using brute force. Quick-witted, charismatic and a natural-born storyteller, you have the capacity to both entertain and inspire your fellow players with your words.

Ranger

Bard

Mostly Es: Mage

In the same way Eleven has spent
her life developing her psychic and
telekinetic abilities, Mages spend
their lives in the study and practice of
magic. As a Mage, you're 'a magic-user
capable of manipulating the structures
of reality', but will you use your powers
for the greater good or will you be
seduced by more selfish or vengeful
reasons? In order to master your arcane
abilities, you must first master yourself.

Mostly Fs: Zoomer

Like Max Mayfield, you're someone
who plays by your own rules. For
example, Zoomer isn't even a real
character class, but why let that stop
you? You have much in common
with the Rogue class – 'a skilled and
resourceful opportunist who uses
stealth and trickery to overcome
obstacles and enemies' – and you
don't mind playing fast and loose with
conventions, expectations and even
morality. You don't necessarily seek
out trouble, but trouble has a way of
finding you …

Mage

Zoomer

CHARACTER PROFILE: MAX MAYFIELD

First things first: don't call her Maxine. Max Mayfield is a talented gamer, a whiz on a skateboard and a dab hand when it comes to stabbing someone with a hypodermic needle. Originally from California, Max moved to Hawkins after her mother married Neil Hargrove (a situation that neither Max nor her stepbrother, Billy, seem too happy about). Max is smart, confident and has a whole lot to prove. (Girls don't play video games? Think again, Dustin.) While she's initially sceptical of the existence of the Upside Down and its terrors, she gets on board thanks to Lucas' efforts and proves herself to be an integral member of the team.

DR MARTIN BRENNER

An evil mastermind and key to Project MKUltra – a CIA-sanctioned research program conducted at Hawkins National Laboratory, intended to develop mind-control techniques in subjects – Dr Brenner is an almost archetypal mad scientist who's big on ambition and sorely lacking in empathy. Dr Brenner styled himself as a father figure to Eleven, manipulating her trust in order to get her to submit to his ongoing experiments. Brenner forces Eleven to test the boundaries of her psychic abilities, leading her to inadvertently open the Gate to the Upside Down. Dr Brenner is cold, sociopathic and ruthless, capable of abducting babies, administering electroshock therapy to grieving mothers, faking a child's dead body, murdering innocent townspeople and unleashing untold horrors into the world, all in the name of science. Dr Brenner was last seen facing the Demogorgon, and it's unclear whether he is dead or alive.

BILLY HARGROVE

Max's stepbrother, Billy, is a classic bully, externalising his inner rage by acting like a jerk to anyone who gets in his way. At best, Billy is a self-obsessed douchebag at worst, he's a violent, racist thug who's capable of acts of great cruelty. Billy terrorises Mike, Dustin and Lucas with his car, forbids his sister to hang out with Lucas and later follows her to the Byers house where he gets into a dramatic fight with Steve Harrington. It's revealed that Billy is the victim of his father's cruelty – we get a tiny glimpse of his humanity, so there may be hope for him yet.

CONNIE FRAZIER

One of Dr Brenner's lackeys, Agent Frazier is a cold-hearted assassin. Impersonating social services in order to intercept Eleven after her escape from Hawkins Lab, she shoots Benny Hammond dead without blinking an eye. Agent Frazier meets a grisly end after a terrified and cornered Eleven crushes her brain using psychic powers.

RAY CARROLL

An orderly at Hawkins National Laboratory, Ray Carroll was involved in the electroshock therapy given to Eleven's mother, Terry Ives – leading to her catatonic state – and was responsible for the cruel treatment of many of the other Project MKUltra test subjects, including Eleven and Kali Prasad (aka Eight). Kali tracks Ray down to exact vengeance, but Eleven shows him mercy after she learns that he has two daughters.

THE MURRAY BAUMAN GAZETTE:

Telling the TRUTH is a Revolutionary Act

EXPOSED: RUSSIAN SPIES AMONG US!

Don't be fooled into thinking that this country is safe from the insidious influence of Russian interference. I've been privy to several disturbing reports of a Russian girl with PSIONIC ABILITIES being spotted in Hawkins. The girl is described as approximately 12 years old, with a shaved head and violent telekinetic abilities. Although the authorities in Hawkins have DENIED ALL KNOWLEDGE, several of my sources have told me the same thing: the Russians are here and the mind control experiments they started with the Nazis in World War II have borne supernatural fruit. Stay alert, citizens. This is only the beginning.

LOOK BEHIND THE CURTAIN: HOW THE GOVERNMENT IS LYING TO YOU

They tell us that we're safe. They tell us there's nothing to worry about. But make no mistake: the government is lying to you. Look at the suspicious amount of security personnel employed by the Department of Energy's National Laboratory in Hawkins. What are they hiding? Last year, a boy named William Byers went missing in Hawkins, and his body – confirmed by AUTOPSY – was pulled out of the Sattler Quarry. But the young Byers boy wasn't dead. In fact, he's alive and well. There's more going on here than meets the eye. And what about Benny Hammond? No enemies. A thriving business. Suddenly he takes his own life. Ask yourself: does this seem ABNORMAL? Is there something in the water? Who knows what experiments they're doing down at the National Laboratory. We've all heard whispers of small towns becoming unwitting test subjects in the government's SECRET BIOLOGICAL EXPERIMENTS. You think it couldn't happen here. But ask yourself: could it?

THE TRUTH ABOUT MIND CONTROL

I've said it once and I'll say it again: the Russians have perfected the mind control techniques that will allow them to launch a SECRET WAR on the US. You won't even realise it's happening. One day you'll just wake up and the President will be doing Russia's dirty work. But there's an even more insidious form of MIND CONTROL at play. The willing participation of US citizens in closing off their minds to the truth. Your priest, your postman, your teacher, the world at large. They won't believe any of this. Most people are completely happy to go through their lives in blissful ignorance. They're not wired like me and you, dear reader. They don't spend their lives trying to get a look at what's behind the curtain. *They like the curtain.* It provides them with stability, comfort, definition. But I'm here to tell you the truth. To open the curtain behind the curtain. To bring you the FACTS about what's going on in our country today.

JUSTICE FOR BARBARA HOLLAND

Imagine for a moment that your daughter goes missing. You're frantic. Desperate. You think maybe she's run away or been ABDUCTED. But what if the truth is even worse than that. What if there are larger forces at work than you knew? This sorry story isn't just a hypothetical. For two Hawkins residents, Mr Holland and his wife, Marsha, this is a nightmare that they live with daily. I'm proud to be investigating the TRUTH behind Barbara Holland's disappearance last year. I've followed up on 200 tips, most of them bogus, but every day I get closer to uncovering who is involved and how they've managed to get away with it. I won't rest until I get JUSTICE for Barb!

EIGHT

CHARACTER PROFILE: EIGHT / KALI PRASAD

Kali Prasad, also known as Eight, is a former 'patient' of Dr Brenner's at Hawkins National Laboratory and current resident of Chicago, Illinois. Kali has powerful psychic abilities, great hair and an axe to grind: she's on a mission to wreak vengeance on the scientists and technicians who hurt her as a child. While she's capable of great violence, she's also deeply protective of the people she loves, including her merry band of misfits (Dottie, Mick, Funshine and Axel) and her spiritual sister, Eleven.

GET EL'S LOOK

ANARCHY IN THE IL

Eleven's dramatic punk makeover (courtesy of her psychic sister, Kali) takes her from Shirley Temple to a latter-day Siouxsie Sioux. From the Madonna-inspired blazer to the slicked-back hair, this is the perfect look for knocking over convenience stores or wreaking vengeance on those who've wronged you.

You can't be an **MTV** punk without smudgy black eyeshadow

A heavy-duty gel tames her curls

The popped collar and rolled sleeves are key

Cuffed jeans are everything

Still rocking the Cons

121

⇜ Stranger Things ⇝
SLANGUAGE

A handy guide to knowing the difference between a wastoid and a weirdo.

Bitchin': An expression of approval or affirmation

Call bull: To expose a lie

Chill: Calm, relaxed, at ease with a situation; the opposite of having a stick up your butt

Curiosity door: Something not yet known; a path to new information

Curiosity voyage: A search for knowledge or, more generally, life itself

Don't cream your pants: Don't get too excited

Douchebag: A derogatory term used to describe someone contemptible or annoying

Freak: A derogatory term used to describe someone eccentric, unusual or socially awkward

Frog Face: A derogatory nickname used by Troy to describe Mike

Got a stick up your butt: When someone is acting uptight, tense or unpleasant; the opposite of chill

Gross: An expression of dismay or disgust

Lando: Short for Lando Calrissian, used to describe a traitor or untrustworthy person

Jock: Someone good at sports; commonly used to describe someone popular and conventional

Mirkwood: Located where the streets Cornwallis and Kerley meet, named after a forest featured in J.R.R. Tolkien's *The Hobbit*

Mouthbreather: A derogatory term used to describe someone stupid and unpleasant

MOUTHBREATHER

MTV punk: A gently mocking term used to describe someone with outlandish dress sense

Pollywog: A scientific term for a tadpole, also used to describe a Demogorgon in its larval stage

Shitbird: A derogatory term used to describe someone irritating

Sissy: A derogatory term used to describe someone cowardly

Stay frosty: Be on the lookout; be alert

Toothless: A derogatory nickname used by Troy to describe Dustin

Totally tubular: An expression of approval; commonly used in California Valley Girl slang

Truesight: Borrowed from *Dungeons & Dragons* terminology, meaning the ability to see into the ethereal plane (in this context, the Upside Down)

Wastoid: A derogatory term used to describe someone as a waste of space or a loser

Weirdo: A derogatory term used to describe someone eccentric, unusual or socially awkward

Wrist-rocket: A hand-powered projectile weapon, commonly known as a slingshot

Your ass is grass: You're in big trouble; there will be consequences to your actions

Zombie Boy: A derogatory nickname used by Hawkins Middle School students to describe Will, in reference to his alleged return from the dead

FLO, CALVIN POWELL & PHIL CALLAHAN

Employees of the Hawkins Police Department. Flo is the sarcastic yet wise Police Department secretary (and the one person who's invested in Hopper's health and wellbeing). Powell is a serious and diligent police officer who remains sceptical despite the mounting level of crazy that is Hawkins, Indiana. Callahan is a surprisingly effective officer despite his cluelessness and career-limiting tendencies to insult his boss and make fun of (albeit deserving) boys who are beaten up by little girls.

NICOLE, CAROL & TOMMY H

Nicole, Carol and Tommy H are Steve Harrington's crew, who enjoy getting drunk by Steve's pool, vandalising public property, picking on outcasts (and destroying their cameras) and generally being obnoxious. Carol and Tommy H are an item and, according to Barb, have been 'having sex since, like, seventh grade'. After they repeatedly insulted Nancy to Steve's face ('The slut with a heart of gold', says Carol), Steve cuts off the friendship. They later find a kindred spirit in Billy.

KEITH

Keith is an acne-encrusted employee of Hawkins arcade parlour, the Palace. Can be easily identified by the bag of Cheetos he's constantly shovelling into his mouth. Has a creepy crush on Nancy.

DONALD MELVALD

Owner of Melvald's General Store where Joyce Byers works. Donald is trying to run a business, but is ultimately a good guy who lets Joyce put her 25 boxes of Christmas lights on credit and only looks at her like she's a little bit insane.

JAMES, TROY & TROY'S MUM

James and Troy are a sociopathic pair of mouthbreathing bullies. Troy pees his pants and then breaks his arm when Eleven uses her powers on him to protect Mike (James just runs away like a big baby). Troy's mum causes a scene at the Hawkins Police Department claiming that a 'psychotic child' broke her son's arm ('A lil' girl, Chief, a lil' one,' Callahan rightly points out).

EARL

A buddy of Benny Hammond, of Benny's Burgers, who knows that Benny's suicide (faked by agents from Hawkins National Laboratory) 'Don't make no sense'.

MERRILL & EUGENE

Merrill is a local Hawkins pumpkin farmer whose entire patch begins to rot. Merrill accuses Eugene, another local farmer, of poisoning his crop. Eugene later returns the accusation. Obviously the destruction is being caused by a series of interconnected tunnels created by a Shadow Monster from a parallel dimension. Why can't they just get along?

MARISSA

Marissa is the very helpful librarian at the Hawkins public library. She and chief Jim Hopper have clearly hooked up.

BRENDA WOOD

Local news anchor and host of *Minute By Minute with Brenda Wood*, a current affairs segment on 5WIYZ, which covered the disappearance of Barb Holland.

DAVID O'BANNON

A trooper for the Indiana State Police, O'Bannon found Will Byers' 'body' in the quarry and is clearly not to be trusted. Chief Jim Hopper confronts him in a bar, like a badass.

THE EMPLOYEES OF HAWKINS NATIONAL LABORATORY

An assortment of general fodder to be variously sent into the Upside Down (to their deaths), to be attacked by the Demogorgon (leading to their deaths) and be generally menacing and/or suspicious.

BARB

CHARACTER PROFILE: BARBARA HOLLAND

Poor Barb. Best friend to Nancy Wheeler, Barb had the misfortune of being in the wrong place at the wrong time and became one of the first people to get pulled into the Upside Down. While the town of Hawkins rallied to search for Will Byers, Barb's disappearance was kind of ignored (and we are *still* mad about it).

Known for her fabulous sense of fashion, sensible nature and unflappable loyalty, Barb was a smart, capable girl who deserved so much better.

#JusticeForBarb

IN MEMORIAM: BARBARA HOLLAND

A senior at Hawkins High School and active in many extracurricular activities, Barbara Holland loved her family and loved her friends. 'She could be reserved, but she had a big heart,' said her mother, Marsha. 'She would go to the ends of the earth for the people she loved.'

Barbara was always 'Barb' to those who knew her best. She excelled academically and was expected to graduate to a good college. It was her ambition to attend an Ivy League school. 'She would have had her pick of any college she wanted,' said Hawkins Senior School's principal. 'She was a bright, ambitious, grounded girl.'

In addition to her academic pursuits, Barbara was also dedicated to community service. She travelled to Indianapolis to participate in a rally against nuclear weapons in June 1982 and volunteered in the clean-up after a blizzard ravaged parts of Hawkins the same year.

'She was kind and thoughtful – a good friend to my daughter and an inspiration to us all,' said resident Karen Wheeler. 'We're heartbroken by her loss.' Nancy Wheeler also expressed her grief. 'She was my best friend; she was always there for me no matter what,' Nancy said. 'She was the kind of friend who'd send you your homework if you'd forgotten about it, the friend that'd remind you when you have an algebra test tomorrow.'

An anonymous accusation, naming several high-ranking members from the US Department of Energy as conspirators in covering up her death, has spurred residents to demand the Hawkins National Laboratory be shut down. 'Our daughter died from exposure to some experimental chemical asphyxiant created by that Lab,' said her father. 'We won't rest until justice is served.'

'She was just such a good person,' said her mother. 'Without her, our family can never be the same.'

QUIZ:

ARE YOU THE ULTIMATE STRANGER THINGS DUNGEON MASTER?

Test your knowledge and claim your place as the true Dungeon Master. How much do you really know about *Stranger Things*?

1) What is Hopper's ex-wife's first name?

2) Which newspaper did Murray Bauman once work for?

3) What is the password to gain entry to Castle Byers?

4) Which member of the Ghostbusters do both Mike and Lucas want to be for Halloween?

5) What is Will's favourite type of candy?

6) For which *Dungeons & Dragons* campaign did Nancy once dress up as an elf?

7) What breed of cat is Tews?

8) What congenital condition does Dustin have?

9) Who are the Wheelers voting for in the 1984 presidential election?

10) Dustin's brontosaurus hoodie is from which museum?

11) How many calories does Hopper's ultimate Eggo extravaganza allegedly contain?

12) Which computer language is Bob Auent in?

13) What brand of cigarettes does Joyce smoke?

14) What is Troy's nickname for Mike?

15) Steve's hairdo is achieved with four puffs of what?

16) Who is Yertle?

17) What are the six phrases that Terry Ives repeats?

18) Complete the sentence: *Mornings are for ...*

19) What is Dart short for, and which book is the name inspired by?

20) According to Nancy, Jonathan's idea of a perfect evening consists of what?

ANSWERS

1) Diane
2) *The Chicago Sun-Times*
3) Radagast
4) Peter Venkman
5) Reese's Pieces
6) The Elder Tree campaign
7) Siamese
8) Cleidocranial dysplasia
9) Ronald Reagan (there's a sign in their front yard)
10) The Science Museum of Minnesota

11) 8000
12) BASIC
13) Camel
14) Frog Face
15) Farrah Fawcett hairspray
16) Dustin's pet turtle
17) Breathe, sunflower, rainbow, three to the right, four to the left, four-fifty
18) ... coffee and contemplation
19) D'Artagnan from *The Three Musketeers*
20) Being home by 8 pm, listening to Talking Heads and reading Kurt Vonnegut

Smith Street Books

Published in 2018 by Smith Street Books
Melbourne | Australia
smithstreetbooks.com

ISBN: 978-1-925418-88-0

CIP data is available from the National Library of Australia.

Publisher: Paul McNally
Project editor: Hannah Koelmeyer
Editor: Ariana Klepac
Design: Stephanie Spartels
Illustration: Phil Constantinesco (Faunesque), The Illustration Room
Stock photography by stock.adobe.com

Printed & bound in China by C&C Offset Printing Co., Ltd.

Book 73
10 9 8 7 6 5 4 3 2 1

Please note: This title is not affiliated in any way with the Netflix series *Stranger Things*. We are just big fans. Please don't sue us.